BIG BRANDS

McDONALD'S
THE BUSINESS BEHIND THE GOLDEN ARCHES

CATH SENKER

Lerner Publications ◆ Minneapolis

contents

the golden arches

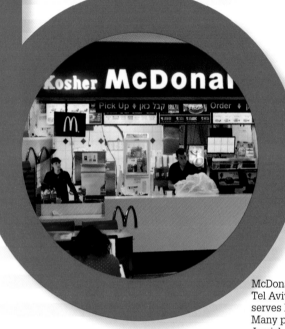

McDonald's in Tel Aviv, Israel, serves kosher food. Many people of the Jewish faith eat kosher diets.

If you find yourself in any major city in the world, chances are that you'll soon spot a McDonald's restaurant. McDonald's is the biggest fast-food chain on the planet, with sales of more than $27 billion in 2014, more than thirty-six thousand outlets, and 1.9 million employees.

McDonald's core products are its classic burgers, shakes, and fries. You could eat a McDonald's cheeseburger anywhere in the world, and it would taste the same. Yet, as well as offering its regular fare, McDonald's also caters to local preferences because more than half of its restaurants are outside the United States. In Brazil, you can buy a quiche de queijo (cheese quiche); red bean pie is available in Hong Kong; and in India, there are plenty of vegetarian options.

This book examines how founder Ray Kroc built McDonald's from a single burger restaurant into a global chain with branches across the world, making it one of the best-known brands worldwide. Although McDonald's is a hugely popular restaurant, the company has been criticized for fueling obesity. If you eat a Big Mac and a large fries with a large Coke, you'll consume 1,430 calories—more than half the daily recommended amount for an adult—and 59 grams (2 ounces) of fat (twice the recommended daily amount). McDonald's has found ways to respond to this criticism, but even with these changes, McDonald's may struggle to stay at the top of the fast-food market.

Business Matters
Diversification

In business, *diversifying* means "adapting to different markets." McDonald's knows that Japanese customers tend to prefer smaller portions than Americans, so the burger you buy in Kyoto is smaller than the one you'd buy in Kansas.

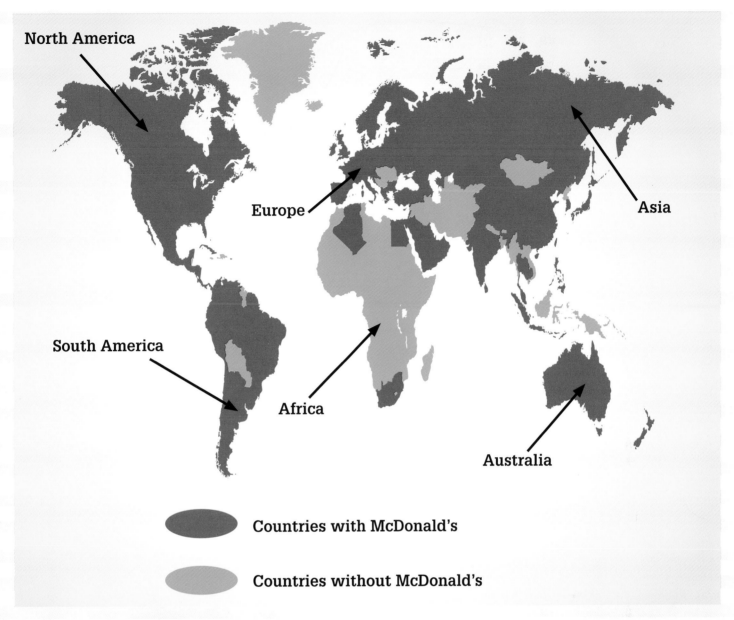

North America

Europe

Asia

South America

Africa

Australia

Countries with McDonald's

Countries without McDonald's

A recent map showing countries with and without McDonald's. Much of Africa has no McDonald's restaurants.

Building the Brand

Brand recognition

Four out of five children recognize the McDonald's logo by the time they are three years old—before some of them even know their own last names.

McDonald's is born

In the United States in the 1940s, as the number of car owners rose, drive-in restaurants became all the rage. Drivers parked and female "carhops" served them in their vehicles. In 1948 Mac and Dick McDonald opened their McDonald's drive-in in San Bernardino, California, providing speedy self-service and cheap burgers. It was hugely popular.

In 1954 salesman Ray Kroc was delighted to receive an order from McDonald's for eight multi-mixers for making milk shakes. When Kroc visited, he found that McDonald's burgers sold for about half the typical price of burgers at other restaurants. Owing to the self-service counter, there was no need to employ carhops. The food was precooked, wrapped, and kept warm under heat lamps so it could be served quickly.

The McDonald brothers weren't interested in expanding the business, but Kroc pitched his big idea to set up McDonald's restaurants all across the country. Mac and Dick agreed—for a fee. In 1955 Kroc founded the McDonald's Corporation and opened his first restaurant in Des Plaines, Illinois. It offered a basic menu of just nine items, including hamburgers, fries, and shakes. Workers made the food on an assembly line, producing burgers that all looked and tasted exactly the same.

The business grew rapidly. In 1958 the company sold its millionth hamburger. Four years later, the first McDonald's restaurant with indoor seating opened in Denver, Colorado, and by 1965, more than seven hundred McDonald's restaurants dotted the United States.

Business Matters
Pricing tactics

Companies may offer a new product at a lower price than their competitors to win sales—Ray Kroc sold his burgers for the bargain price of fifteen cents. This pricing strategy is called penetration.

The McDonald brothers' original restaurant in San Bernadino, California

Ray Kroc

McDonald's founder, president, and chair (1955-1984)

Ray Kroc was an ambitious businessman—from early on, he said that he intended to open one thousand McDonald's restaurants. The secret of his business model was offering food of consistently high quality, with good service, and in a clean environment. For example, the hamburger meat had to be exactly centered on the bun, and the restaurant facilities, especially the restrooms, had to be spotless.

> **If I had a brick for every time I've repeated the phrase Quality, Service, Cleanliness, and Value, I think I'd probably be able to bridge the Atlantic Ocean with them.**
>
> Ray Kroc, *Grinding It Out*, 1977

Customers at Ray Kroc's first McDonald's in Des Plaines, Illinois, in 1955

McDonald's across the world

Kroc developed the McDonald's look so his restaurants would be instantly recognizable. In 1969 the bright yellow Golden Arches logo was made more prominent and became the key symbol of McDonald's.

The original menu was expanded to bring in more customers. In 1975 McDonald's restaurant owner Herb Peterson of Santa Barbara, California, invented the Egg McMuffin to entice people to have breakfast at McDonald's. A clever marketing manager thought, "Why not have a meal just for children?" and in 1979, Happy Meals were born. When children opened the box, they found a toy nestled in with their burger, fries, and cookies.

McDonald's went international too. In 1967 branches opened in Canada and Puerto Rico, and by 1983, there were McDonald's restaurants in thirty-two countries.

A McDonald's Happy Meal in its bright, appealing box

Building the Brand
Giving back to the community

Russians lined up on the day that McDonald's opened in Moscow.

Business Matters

Logos and slogans

Companies devise logos and slogans and use them across all their stores and publicity so consumers recognize them instantly. The McDonald's Golden Arches logo and the slogan I'm Lovin' It are among the best-known in the world.

As communism fell in Eastern Europe, McDonald's was seen as a symbol of the Western lifestyle. On the day that the first McDonald's opened in Moscow, Russia, in 1990, more than thirty thousand customers lined up for burgers!

Yet in the late twentieth century, the company expanded too quickly. In 2002 McDonald's made a loss for the first time. As Chief Executive Officer Jim Skinner noted, this was the year of the "perfect storm" when everything went wrong. McDonald's had been opening two thousand stores a year, an unmanageable level of growth that had resulted in a lack of attention to basics. Customers complained about dirty stores, cold food, and unfriendly staff. Skinner's strategy was to slow down growth and improve the existing stores, focusing on cleanliness and efficient service. The kitchens were revamped, and food was made fresh to order. More chicken and salad dishes were introduced to provide more healthful options.

It is good for a business's image to undertake charity work, and Kroc wanted to show that McDonald's gave back to communities. In 1974 the first Ronald McDonald House opened. This charity offered free accommodations for families who had children in the hospital. As of 2014, there were houses in sixty-two countries around the world—including this one in the Netherlands.

the fast-food revolution

Young people enjoy malt drinks at a US café in the 1950s.

McDonald's achieved success because it started out in the right place at the right time. After World War II (1939–1945), a new fast-food culture developed in Western countries. Economies were expanding, wages were rising, and more people had cars. They had leisure time and money to spend, so going out to eat became a favorite pastime. Fast-food chains such as McDonald's, Burger King, and Kentucky Fried Chicken grew rapidly.

The industry was revolutionized by innovation in food preparation technology. Assembly-line production was introduced so skilled chefs were not required—each worker in the line followed strict instructions to do one task, such as frying the burger patties. Many of the customers bought takeout food and did not use the restaurant facilities, reducing the company's costs further. Self-service fast-food outlets put many traditional restaurants out of business.

Chains such as McDonald's and Burger King were family friendly—cheerful, bright, and air-conditioned, with clean restrooms. They also proved popular with working people eating alone as burgers and fries made a cheap, quick meal for lunch breaks.

The restaurants spread quickly because of franchising. McDonald's was one of the leaders in introducing franchising, in which owner-operators purchased the restaurants and ran them. Franchising used the benefits of the company's management and systems and linked them to local businesspeople who invested their own money in the restaurants.

> **While the Company's menu is limited, it contains food staples [basics] that are widely accepted in North America. It is for these reasons that demand for its products is less sensitive to economic fluctuations [changes] than most other restaurant formats.**
>
> **Ray Kroc, explaining why fast-food restaurants are so popular, 1977**

Market Shares of the Major Players in the Fast-Food Industry

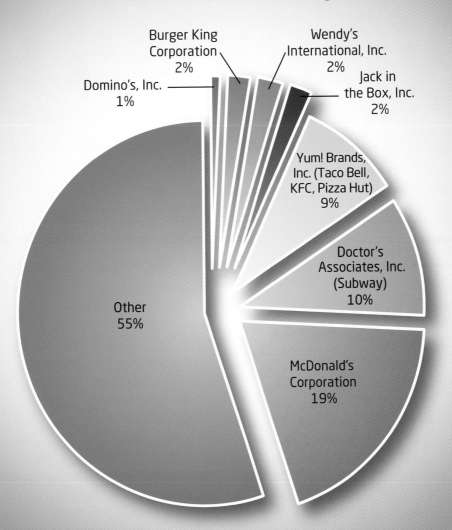

Burger King Corporation
2%

Wendy's International, Inc.
2%

Domino's, Inc.
1%

Jack in the Box, Inc.
2%

Yum! Brands, Inc. (Taco Bell, KFC, Pizza Hut)
9%

Doctor's Associates, Inc. (Subway)
10%

Other
55%

McDonald's Corporation
19%

A 2012 chart showing the market shares at that time of companies in the US fast-food industry

A server takes orders at an early drive-through restaurant.

Business Matters
Product life cycle

Every product goes through these stages: introduction, growth, maturity, and decline. As products decline, they are withdrawn and new ones are introduced—this is the product life cycle. According to McDonald's, the Big Mac is probably at the maturity stage.

"in business for yourself but not by yourself"

McDonald's workers serve coffee at a McCafé outlet in Illinois.

Kroc built McDonald's on the principle of the "three-legged stool"— the McDonald's Corporation, the franchisees, and the suppliers together were the key to success. He told franchisees that "[you are] in business for yourself, but not by yourself."

Most McDonald's restaurants are run under the franchise system. Today there are more than three thousand owner-operators in the United States. If you're thinking of setting up as a US franchisee, you'll need a minimum investment of around $750,000—and 25 percent ($187,500) has to be paid up front (the rest can be borrowed). So you need to be quite wealthy to begin with! McDonald's focuses on countries where it already has restaurants and keeps a list of countries

Business Matters
Training

Companies train their staff to work according to the business's standards. In 1961 McDonald's opened Hamburger University at Elk Grove Village, Illinois, to instruct franchisees and operators how to run a McDonald's restaurant.

One of more than sixty McDonald's restaurants in Miami, Florida

where it is seeking franchisees. You'll need to check if your country is one of them.

The franchisees all have to follow McDonald's core values of quality, service, cleanliness, and value. But they are free to develop their own ideas to improve the business. It was franchisees who came up with the Big Mac, the Filet-O-Fish, and the Egg McMuffin.

Although individuals run the branches, all McDonald's products must be identical everywhere. For example, all suppliers making a cheeseburger have to match a target product. All the ingredients, such as the seasonings, are tested and tasted, with testers making notes after every bite. If the taste doesn't match the target, the supplier has to try again until it does.

Fred Turner
head of operations, 1957-1968

Fred Turner was always thinking of ways to make the McDonald's operation faster. He asked bakers to provide individual burger buns already sliced all the way through, rather than in clusters of four or six. Turner also wrote the McDonald's handbook, which explained every detail of all McDonald's production methods. For instance, french fries had to be cut precisely 0.28 inches (0.7 centimeters) thick. He also pushed for franchisees to be involved in running stores rather than just investing in them—a very successful strategy.

Fred Turner rose from cook to the top of McDonald's.

bringing in the children

Another key to McDonald's success is the way it attracts children to its restaurants. In the United States, children aged two to eleven see more than twice the number of McDonald's ads than those of its competitors.

Children are an easy target since research shows that children under eight often do not realize that an ad is trying to sell them something. They believe what they see is true. McDonald's ads tell them that Happy Meals are perfect for children, so they may ask their parents to take them to McDonald's.

It's the toys that are the major attraction of Happy Meals, though. A successful toy promotion can double or triple the number of children's meals McDonald's sells in a week. Often McDonald's distributes a set of toys so children make repeat visits to collect them all.

> **"The restaurant chain [McDonald's] evoked a series of pleasing images in a youngster's mind:** bright colors, a playground, a toy, a clown, a drink with a straw, little pieces of food wrapped up like a present. **"**
>
> **Eric Schlosser, *Fast Food Nation*, 2001**

When challenged about marketing high-fat fast food to children, McDonald's replies that it promotes healthful options in its ads for children, focusing on fruit, vegetables, and milk. The restaurants sell more of these healthful items than ever before.

Happy Meal toys are often characters from popular movies.

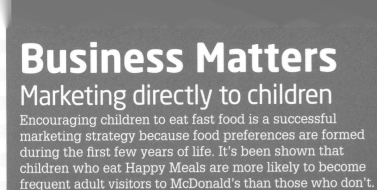

Business Matters

Marketing directly to children

Encouraging children to eat fast food is a successful marketing strategy because food preferences are formed during the first few years of life. It's been shown that children who eat Happy Meals are more likely to become frequent adult visitors to McDonald's than those who don't.

Building the Brand

Ronald McDonald

In the 1960s, the McDonald's marketing team decided the company needed a child-friendly character to attract young visitors, and they put huge efforts into creating the Ronald McDonald clown. In 1966 Ronald appeared in his first national TV ad. With his bright appearance and friendly personality, he was an instant hit. He continues to represent the brand to this day, and McDonald's claims Ronald McDonald is one of the most recognizable characters on the planet, second only to Santa!

Getting into the soccer spirit at the McDonald's World Cup launch party in New York, 2014

Business Matters

Marketing alliances

A marketing alliance is an agreement between two companies to promote each other's products.

big brand tie-ins

Popular children's characters Woody and Buzz Lightyear deliver Happy Meals at McDonald's in Tokyo, Japan.

McDonald's has often made marketing alliances with other big brands to encourage customers to link a favorite drink, activity, or sport with its food.

Since 1955 McDonald's has had a marketing agreement with Coca-Cola to sell its drinks in all McDonald's outlets. Burgers, fries, and Coke make a perfect combination, which is highly profitable for both companies—about 5 percent of McDonald's profits come from the sale of soft drinks. However, the company has been criticized for selling large cup sizes of sugary drinks with its meals.

In 1996 McDonald's made a ten-year global marketing agreement with entertainment company Disney. McDonald's outlets opened at Disney theme parks, and children were excited to find toys linked to the latest Disney movie in Happy Meals. This was a clever marketing strategy. McDonald's knew that parents took their children to McDonald's because they wanted to feel like good parents and make the kids happy— and it was far cheaper than visiting a Disney theme park. The ads proclaimed, "Only McDonald's makes it easy to get a bit of Disney magic." But Disney refused to renew the deal in 2006, preferring to distance itself from fast food because of the dramatic rise in obesity.

The restaurant giant's links with high-profile sports events continue, though. During the 2014 World Cup, McDonald's Gol! program ("gol" means "goal" in Portuguese) asked twelve artists from around the world to create soccer-related designs on french fry boxes. Customers could hold their cell phone to the box to download an app with a game involving "kicking" a ball by flicking a finger.

Roy Bergold
chief creative officer (a. 1972–2001)

Faced with falling sales in the early 2000s, McDonald's hoped to rebuild the emotional link people felt with the company by reminding them of how they'd loved McDonald's in the past. Roy Bergold was in charge of the marketing campaign, writing that "the challenge of the campaign is to make customers believe that McDonald's is their 'Trusted Friend.'" The company made alliances with other big brands, such as Disney, so that customers would associate enjoyable events with McDonald's and feel that the company knew their needs and cared about them.

connecting with customers

Just as McDonald's marketing alliances create a positive image of the brand, its direct marketing to customers focuses on their feelings, so when they arrive hungry in a new city, the idea of McDonald's immediately pops into their heads.

Customers clearly do link fast food with the McDonald's brand. In 2014 it was the top fast-food brand in the list of most valuable global brands compiled by BrandZ (a company that ranks the world's leading brands).

Yet McDonald's cannot rely on its brand reputation alone and uses all kinds of media to spread its message. Online, it hosts a separate website for each country and tailors its sites to different communities. In the United States, it has websites for children; Me Encanta for Spanish speakers; 365Black, catering to African Americans; and a site for the Asian Pacific American community.

The public can have a two-way conversation with the restaurant giant through all major social media sites in different countries. But McDonald's has experienced some difficulties with social media. The company has been criticized for simply putting out advertising rather than providing the useful, interesting content that fans expect from social media. Also, on Twitter, it receives lots of negative mentions focusing on the unhealthful nature of its core products, a major issue for McDonald's.

Clever marketing to hungry drivers in Minnesota

Business Matters
Promotion

Promotion falls into two main categories:

1. Ads that are on TV, at the theater, online, and in posters, the press, and social media. These aim to make people aware of the product and feel positive about it.
2. Sales promotions through displays, direct mail, merchandising (selling goods linked to a popular movie or event), telemarketing (selling by phone), exhibitions, and loyalty programs. These focus on persuading people to buy the product or buy more of it and recommend it to others.

A customer surfs the Internet with a high-speed wireless connection at a McDonald's in San Francisco, California.

Building the Brand

Market research

McDonald's does market research on its target customers, which it calls key audiences. It explores what appeals to them at McDonald's, so the company can advertise to them effectively. These are its findings:

- Parents go to McDonald's to give the kids a treat.
- Children want to go because it's fun, and they like the toys in Happy Meals.
- Businesspeople can eat a quick meal there during the day.
- Teenagers like the affordable Dollar Menu and Wi-Fi access.

fast food and obesity

In countries where people regularly eat fast food, the obesity rate has risen alarmingly. For example, in the United States and United Kingdom, childhood obesity rates have more than tripled since 1980. In newer fast-food markets, including China and Japan, obesity is increasing.

Is McDonald's to blame? Many health experts believe it contributes to the obesity crisis. Both the fat content and portion size of its food have risen. In the 1950s, just one burger size was sold, but now, far larger portions are offered cheaply. The double quarter pounder burger contains 500 percent more hamburger meat than the original size. A serving of fries has increased by 250 percent. For his 2009 documentary, *Super Size Me*, filmmaker Morgan Spurlock lived on McDonald's food alone for a month, and his health suffered badly from the high-fat, high-sugar content of the diet.

Some meals that customers think are good for them contain a lot of fat. Chicken nuggets were introduced in 1983. They appeared to be more healthful than burgers because they were made from chicken rather than red meat. But the meat comes from factory-farmed chickens that are kept in small cages and grow fat. A portion of chicken today contains 50 percent more calories than it did in 1970.

In response, McDonald's claims that people don't eat its meals frequently enough to damage their health. It says people have to make their own decisions about what they eat, and healthful options are always available. Yet most people who go to McDonald's choose a burger and fries and have no idea of the calorie content of their meals—few read the calorie information on the wrappers.

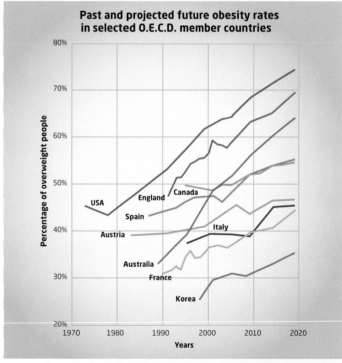

A graph from the Organisation for Economic Co-operation and Development shows that obesity rates in several countries are continuing to rise.

> **"** Evidence shows that if people are served larger portions, they'll eat larger portions! **"**
>
> **Kelly Brownell, director of Yale University's Rudd Center for Food Policy and Obesity**

Business Matters
Responding to criticism

Companies may make changes to their products in response to negative publicity. After Morgan Spurlock's documentary, McDonald's scrapped its supersize portions, and to date, they have not been brought back.

Morgan Spurlock (*below*) put on weight and suffered liver damage while eating McDonald's food alone.

countering the health critics

Dan Coudreaut
head of culinary innovation (from 2004)

Known as Chef Dan, Dan Coudreaut is in charge of developing new menu items for McDonald's. He's the brains behind dishes at McDonald's such as the Southwest salad, made with fire-roasted corn, savory black beans, poblano peppers, tortilla strips, and lime. To cater to the popular habit of grazing—having five small meals rather than three larger ones—he developed the Snack Wrap, with beef or chicken wrapped in a soft tortilla. All of Chef Dan's new recipes have to be easy for crews to make in the restaurants. Not all McDonald's innovations are successful, though. There have been some famous failures, such as the McPizza, which flopped badly because it took too long to bake.

McDonald's has made efforts to offer customers more healthful options such as fresh salads and low-fat desserts alongside its traditional burgers, fries, and Coke.

The company still focuses on marketing to children because families form a large part of the customer base. But Happy Meals now include a child-sized portion of fries, fruit or yogurt, and fruit juice or milk instead of Coke. The website does not promote fries to children—it advertises fruity treats such as apple slices.

Another venture is McCafé. Introduced in 2009, this adult-orientated McDonald's coffee bar focuses on coffee and fruit smoothies rather than fast food and offers lower prices than coffee chains like Starbucks.

McDonald's states that it aims to include more fruit and vegetables in its menu and less salt, sugar, and unhealthful fats. There is evidence that McDonald's is ahead of rival burger chains in this goal. Yet as obesity expert Kelly Brownell comments, McDonald's still offers a "tidal wave of bad food with a few drops of goodness."

Pick Up ↓ קבל כאן

קבלת מוצרים

Order

Business Matters

Research and development (R&D)

The food industry continually needs to innovate to keep up with eating trends. The R&D departments of food companies carry out market research to investigate consumers' eating habits and develop new menu items they believe will be popular.

workers and the environment

Battery chickens in cramped conditions

> **The production of much of the raw products which go into McDonald's meals, from burger patties to sauces, is subcontracted to different suppliers, making it impossible to assess the company in terms of a single golden standard.**
>
> **Peter Salisbury, Global Research, 2014**

As well as being criticized for its unhealthful foods, McDonald's has been blamed for treating its staff badly and harming the environment. In the United States, for example, many frontline fast-food workers earn very low wages. In the United Kingdom, 90 percent of McDonald's staff work on zero-hours contracts—they only find out at the start of each week how many hours they will work.

McDonald's doesn't take criticism lightly. Between 1994 and 1997, the company sued UK environmental activists Helen Steel and Dave Morris for distributing pamphlets criticizing the company. The pair were unable to prove all of their claims against McDonald's, but the judge eventually agreed that it exploited children, falsely said its food was nutritious, indirectly sponsored cruelty to animals, and paid low wages. This was a blow to the brand.

Since the early 2000s, McDonald's has made progress in introducing ethical and eco-friendly practices. In the United Kingdom, for example, burgers are now made with 100 percent beef with no preservatives or added flavors.

Yet the advances are limited. The huge cattle herds that provide meat for McDonald's give off methane, which is a greenhouse gas, or gas that contributes to global warming. In the United States, cattle are often factory farmed—that is, huge numbers of cows are kept in crowded conditions.

McDonald's does not have complete control over where its meat and other supplies come from because 80 percent of outlets are run by franchisees. The franchisees have to follow the laws of the countries they're based in, and some countries don't have strict rules to protect the environment. So whether McDonald's suppliers are eco-friendly or not may depend on the country or franchisee.

A McDonald's crew busy at work in Beijing, China

Business Matters
Eco-friendly efforts
It's important for the reputation of big brands to try to be more eco-friendly. For example, 80 percent of McDonald's packaging is recycled.

hamburgers forever

McDonald's has proved highly successful in China.

Around 2000 McDonald's experimented with buying other kinds of food outlets, including Donatos Pizza and Pret A Manger (a coffee and sandwich shop). But it sold them again within a few years. In the future, McDonald's is likely to stick to its core business—as CEO Steve Easterbrook said, "Everyone likes a burger every now and then."

Having overextended itself in the past, the company is wary of expanding too quickly. But it's likely to continue to grow in international markets, particularly in China, where it already has around two thousand restaurants, and in African countries too.

McDonald's will have to cope with competition, particularly from "fast casual" chains such as Subway, Five Guys, and Chipotle, which offer a more healthful, fresher, and more varied menu. To counter these chains, McDonald's plans to invest in remodeling its stores and introducing mobile ordering and payments.

To stay ahead of its competition, McDonald's will keep an eye on people's changing eating habits and their economic situations and alter its products accordingly. McDonald's will be sure to offer plenty of value options for cash-strapped customers. The menu has grown by 70 percent since 2007, and franchisees say this creates more work and costs, so it's likely the range of items will be reduced. Salads and fruit desserts will always be available, but most customers will no doubt continue to visit McDonald's for the all-American meal of burgers, fries, and Coke.

Business Matters
Cross-selling

Cross-selling is encouraging a customer who has already bought an item to buy another one—for example, the famous McDonald's sales line: "Do you want fries with that?" It is effective if the salesperson suggests an item that goes well with the customer's original choice.

Fast-food outlets are growing in popularity in the Middle East—this McDonald's is in Dubai, United Arab Emirates.

Five Guys is one of the United States' fastest-growing burger chains. It runs on a similar franchising system to McDonald's.

Building the Brand

McDonald's in the Middle East

In many Middle Eastern countries, people resent the influence of US culture, but McDonald's has succeeded in adapting its message to show that the company respects local customs. Muslims do not eat meat from pigs, so in countries with large Muslim populations, McDonald's uses no pork or ham. All meat is halal, or from animals that have been killed according to Islamic dietary rules. In Oman a menu item called the Share Box is sold for families, to fit with the Middle Eastern tradition of sharing food from a central dish.

market a new McDonald's line

When you create a fantastic new product, you need to come up with a marketing strategy to sell it. Here's a sample marketing strategy for a possible line. Why not see if you can come up with your own idea for a new McDonald's menu item?

McTea Time

Expanding on the development of McCafé, McDonald's can exploit the popularity of tea drinking in many countries and bring in new customers who do not normally eat at McDonald's.

Stage 1: Work out your objectives

Step 1. Make sure they fit with your corporate strategy.
Selling tea along with low-fat and low-sugar treats fits with McDonald's strategy to offer more healthful items.

Step 2. What do you hope to achieve?
Research shows that many people prefer to graze on five smaller meals. The teatime offering will bring in customers for another meal at McDonald's.

Stage 2: Product detail

Step 1. Product description and positioning
What is it?
A variety of tea flavors will be offered, including traditional teas and herbal alternatives, accompanied by low-fat, low-sugar, and gluten-free cookies and snacks.

Who is it for?
Target customers will be people who may not be attracted by the regular McDonald's menu but are looking for a low-priced venue for light refreshments.

What's the benefit?
The McTea Time menu provides a more healthful alternative to high-sugar soft drinks.

Evidence to support your claims
The successful introduction of McCafé indicates that there is a market for hot drinks and snacks.

Step 2. How will it be different from other products?
Light, teatime treats not on the current McCafé or dessert menu will be introduced.

Step 3. What is the pricing policy?
As with McCafé, tea prices will be lower than at competitors' cafes such as Starbucks. The markup on tea (extra amount charged, above the cost of making it) served in cafés is very high, so even with a lower price, the venture will still be profitable.

Step 4. What's the unique selling proposition (USP)?
McTea Time will be available all day at a lower price than at rival cafés.

Stage 3: Understand the market
Step 1. Figure out which niche gives the best sales possibilities
McTea Time will be launched first in markets where the tea-drinking habit is well-established.

Step 2. Create customer profiles
Market research will identify groups that currently do not tend to go to McDonald's but could be encouraged to make use of the McTea Time offer.

Stage 4: Check the competition
What competition is there likely to be?
There are many established café chains as well as independent tea shops. McDonald's would need to offer good value to attract customers away from its rivals.

Stage 5: Build your sales plan
Step 1. Key messages
The key message will focus on the low price, the convenience of McTea Time, and the healthful accompanying snacks.

Step 2. Promotion
The promotion strategy will include advertising in traditional media—the press, TV, theaters, and billboards. The public relations team will offer features about McTea Time on its website, and there will be a social media and mobile marketing campaign. Promotions to engage customers will include "tea tryouts" with vouchers for free tea and snacks.

Stage 6: Launch!
High-profile launch events will be held in all key target markets, with free tea for customers on launch day.

glossary

alliance
in business, an agreement between two companies to work together for the benefit of both of them

assembly line
A line of workers and machines carrying out a process. Each worker does his or her part of the job and passes the product on to the next person in the line.

brand
a type of product made by a particular company

calorie
a unit for measuring how much energy food will produce

chain
a group of shops or restaurants owned by the same company

communism
the system of government in the former Soviet Union (1922–1991) under which the state controlled the means of producing everything

ethical
Morally right. In business, it means treating people, animals, and the environment well.

franchising
Permission given by a company to somebody who wants to sell its goods or services in a particular area. The person who runs the business is called a franchisee.

frontline fast-food workers
the people who work directly with customers

global warming
the rise in temperature of Earth's atmosphere that is caused by the increase of gases such as carbon dioxide and methane

innovation
the introduction of new things, ideas, or ways of doing something

invest
to put money into a business in the hope of making a profit

logo
a printed design or symbol that a company or an organization uses as its special sign

loss
when a business loses money instead of making it

marketing
presenting, advertising, and selling a company's products in the best possible way

obesity
the condition of being very overweight

outlet
a shop or restaurant that sells goods made by a particular company or of a particular type

preservative
a substance used to prevent food from decaying

promotion
activities done to increase the sales of a product or service

publicity
the business of attracting the attention of the public to something, such as a new product

reputation
the opinion that people have about something, such as a product, based on what has happened in the past

slogan
A word or phrase that is easy to remember. It is often used in advertising to attract people's attention or to suggest an idea quickly.

zero-hours contract
when a company does not employ workers for a fixed number of hours per week but tells them each week how many hours they will work

further information

Print

Schlosser, Eric. *Chew on This: Everything You Don't Want to Know about Fast Food.* Boston: Houghton Mifflin, 2006.

Web

Fast Food Factory
http://www.bbc.co.uk/worldservice/specials/1616_fastfood/index.shtml

Happy Meals
http://www.happymeal.com

Marketing at McDonald's
http://www.mcdonalds.co.uk/content/dam/McDonaldsUK/People/
Schools-and-students/mcd_marketing.pdf

McDonald's
http://www.mcdonalds.com

McDonald's Abroad
http://content.time.com/time/world/article/0,8599,1932839,00.html

Videos

"Big Mac: Inside the McDonald's Empire"
http://www.youtube.com/watch?v=J4a4r-Iyf10

"Ray Kroc Documentary McDonald's History"
http://www.youtube.com/watch?v=k7bivuNlbi0

Spurlock, Morgan. *Super Size Me.* DVD.
Culver City, CA, Sony Pictures, 2004.

index

First American edition published in 2016 by Lerner Publishing Group, Inc.
First published in 2015 by Wayland

Copyright © 2015 Wayland, a division of Hachette Children's Group,
an Hachette UK company
published by arrangement with Wayland

Lerner Publications Company
A division of Lerner Publishing Group, Inc.
241 First Avenue North
Minneapolis, MN 55401 USA

For reading levels and more information, look up this title at www.lernerbooks.com.

Main body text set in Glypha LT Std. Typeface provided by Adobe Systems.

Library of Congress Cataloging-in-Publication Data

Senker, Cath, author.
    McDonald's : the business behind the Golden Arches / by Cath Senker.
        pages cm. — (Big brands)
    Audience: Ages 9–12.
    Audience: Grades 4 to 6.
    Summary: "How did the McDonald's logo become an iconic symbol for
fast, inexpensive meals? Discover how McDonald's grew from one hamburger
restaurant to one of the world's largest restaurant chains."— Provided by
publisher.
    Includes bibliographical references and index.
    ISBN 978-1-5124-0590-3 (lb : alk. paper) — ISBN 978-1-5124-0593-4 (EB pdf)
    1. Kroc, Ray, 1902–1984—Juvenile literature. 2. McDonald's Corporation—
Juvenile literature. 3. Fast food restaurants—Juvenile literature. 4.
Convenience foods—Juvenile literature. I. Title.
TX945.5.M33S46 2016
338.7'6164795—dc23   2015033981

Manufactured in the United States of America
1 – VI – 12/31/15

Photo Acknowledgments
Cover: tehcheesiong/Shutterstock.com (top), Bikeworldtravel/Shutterstock.
com (bottom); p1: iStockphoto.com/EdStock (top), The Image Works/TopFoto
(bottom); p4: Boris-B/Shutterstock.com; p5: Stefan Chabluk (top), 360b/
Shutterstock.com (bottom); p6: Photoshot; p7: Everett Collection/REX (bottom),
Art Shay/The LIFE Images Collection/Getty Images (top); p8: BikeWorldTravel/
Shutterstock.com (top), tehcheesiong/Shutterstock.com (bottom); p9: Photoshot/
TopFoto (top), hans engbers/Shutterstock.com (bottom); p10: H. Armstrong
Roberts/ClassicStock/Topfoto; p11: Stefan Chabluk (top); Everett Collection/
REX (bottom); p12: Action Press/ REX; p13: Alexanderphoto7 (top), Mark
Peterson/Corbis (bottom left), Photoshot; p14: iStock/EdStock (left), Paisan
Homhuan (right); p15: The Image Works/TopFoto; p16: Neilson Barnard/Getty
Images for McDonald's; p17: Kurita KAKU/Gamma-Rapho via Getty Images;
p18: iStock/skhoward; p19: Justin Sullivan/Getty Images; p20: Stefan Chabluk;
p21: Jakub Cejpek/Shutterstock.com (top), Snap Stills/REX (bottom); p22:
Daniel Acker/Bloomberg via Getty Images; p23: Boris-B/Shutterstock.com; p24:
branislavpudar/Shutterstock.com (left), Creative Nature Media/Shutterstock.com
(right); p25: American Spirit/Shutterstock.com; p26: dailin/Shutterstock.com;
p27: Michael Luhrenberg/iStock (top), Ken Wolter/Shutterstock.com (bottom);
p28: saknakorn/Shutterstock.com; p29: Africa Studio/Shutterstock.com.